Memory House
OF LOVE AND DEMENTIA

L. G. MASON

Copyright © 2025 L. G. Mason.

All rights reserved. No part of this book may be reproduced, stored, or transmitted by any means—whether auditory, graphic, mechanical, or electronic—without written permission of both publisher and author, except in the case of brief excerpts used in critical articles and reviews. Unauthorized reproduction of any part of this work is illegal and is punishable by law.

ISBN: 979-8-89419-625-1 (sc)
ISBN: 979-8-89419-626-8 (hc)
ISBN: 979-8-89419-627-5 (e)

Because of the dynamic nature of the Internet, any web addresses or links contained in this book may have changed since publication and may no longer be valid. The views expressed in this work are solely those of the author and do not necessarily reflect the views of the publisher, and the publisher hereby disclaims any responsibility for them.

One Galleria Blvd., Suite 1900, Metairie, LA 70001
(504) 702-6708

The memoir becomes both a repository for these remembrances and a place to ruminate on the complex mix of grief, guilt, love, and longing that roils in his mind. Mason's prose is stark and lyrical, boiled down into gutting statements and concise descriptions...It's a slim work at under 70 pages, but the author's voice is so enchanting that readers will feel their throats clench after only a few paragraphs. Though the situation is surely a common one, Mason confronts it with a grasping vulnerability that is both endearing and devastating. It's an affecting rumination on the impossibility of mourning someone who hasn't yet died.

—*Kirkus Reviews*

Together my love, we walk in the gardens at Memory House. You point at the colors. You celebrate the blue sky and the height of the spruces. You count the birds and the clouds. You pick flowers off the manicured shrubs and back in your room, you put them in paper cups with a little water.

Sometimes you tell me you want to go home. But home is not mostly a place. Home is a time. Or a hole in time. You want to go home to your grandmother's kitchen on Spring Street in Albany, sixty or seventy years ago. Your mama's there. and Aunt Dorothy. They'll laugh with you again, and hear you sing and play the piano. They'll poke fun again at your latest boyfriend.

When you and I lived together, not so long ago, I fed you, kept our place in tolerable order, and washed your clothes. You folded them and chose sometimes which ones to wear. I listened to your dreams. And told you, when you asked me, what I could remember: how we'd met, when we married, who our children were. You'd ask about your cats: "How many do I have? Tell me all their names."

Couldn't put you in a home. Couldn't be without you and stay sane. Kept you in that house with me, to satisfy my selfish craving after warmth and sanity.

Until you pulled away, until you wouldn't let me dress you, give you pills or keep you clean. Or keep you safe. You hated me for trying. With a fury and a venom. I could not believe you hated me.

And I've let them take you away. Now I can forget you for an hour or two. Now I come to see you and I tell you no, we can't run off together, no, I can't stay with you. And you tell me I don't love you anymore.

But I did the right thing. Everyone agrees. For the sake of your health and your safety. As old as both of us are, what the hell is the point of health and safety? But I didn't say that.

I let them take you away. I couldn't face your hatred anymore.

The other day I looked at you and couldn't find you. Got so used to you the way you are. You were standing there in front of me and I couldn't picture who you used to be.

I panicked. Started going through the stuff I used to put on paper. Notes and poems and god-knows-what. And things you said, that I remembered and wrote down.

And I started putting whatever-this-is together.

And you're coming into focus: a rescuer and a keeper of strays. A fierce defender of what was yours, a lover or hater with equal passion.
You never could bear to lose anything. To lose a houseplant, say, or lose a cat. My god, to lose a cat! One of them just took off one day and never came back. You saw him in the neighborhood a few times afterward, but he never came to the door again.

Or to lose your favorite and best piano student, when it was time for him to move on. Or (god knows) a daughter, when she grew up.

A teacher, a merciless teacher, a terror with a piano:
"You've never played?"
"No," somebody would say.
"It's easy, come I'll show you."
"No, really, I…"
"Sit down for god's sake. You can't play standing up."
"I'm not very good at this sort of…"
"Just put your hands like this. No, like this."
"I really don't have any talent for…"
"It's easy, you'll see. We'll start with the key of C. We won't do the black keys right away."

A fool for adventure. Like one of your cats with a ball. Never letting your world stop spinning. Poking at it whenever it came to rest. I could never keep up with you. You never stayed still long enough. I stood or sat in one place while your voice and your mind and your body flew by.

"We're so different," you used to tell me . I would get reflective about it. I'd wax pedantic: "That's a good thing" I'd say. "People who are different bring things to each other that they never would have found alone." I'd look up and you'd be gone.

"The way you touch me," you told me once, "I think I must be beautiful."
And then you added, "But you never tell me so."
I shrugged. "You're beautiful."
You standing at your mirror: "Well maybe, if you just look at the head and shoulders."

"You're beautiful," I said again, to shut you up.
"You're a pain in the ass," you said.

You also said once, "You don't love me enough."
I used to shut myself away for hours with my words and my wine and leave you alone. I guess that's what you meant. Anyway I wasn't the ardent, drunken young fool who used to pursue you. Though I was still a drunk and still a fool and god knows I still loved you. But you married me not knowing how much I also loved the wine and the words.

One morning I lay by your side, haunted by images out of a dream, wanting to slip out of bed and get them on paper. But then you touched me. I kissed you and put my hand to your face and held you in my arms and we stayed a long time together, while images spilled over the dawn like precious oil, and I lost them forever. I lay by your side, wondering whether I loved you enough.

But you forgave me. I forgave you too, for knowing how not to be alone.

I even (when it almost stopped hurting) became your confessor. You brought your life to me, almost Catholic sometimes in your penitence. I was almost priestly with forgiveness. You afterward returned to your temptation. I went back (priestly) to my wine.

I come these days to Memory House and you talk for hours, and make no sense, except when you tell me you want to go where I can't take you. Finally I escape, but next day I'll want to be with you. Meanwhile, I stay in the house we shared, and wash the dishes and pay the bills and feed the cats. Meanwhile I get the CD's ready to bring to your room so we can listen together. (That part of it both of us love.)
And I wait, longing to see you again.

On a good day, you love everyone. But on the nights and the days of the worst of your pain, it's their fault: the people around you. "I hate them all," you tell me. "I won't stay here another day."

You tell me why you hurt. You never mention your twisted spine, your back held together with rods and screws. You tell me about the man who threw the darkness on you, and the people who come in the night and break you, over and over again.

You gave them an awful time at first, at Memory House. Wouldn't get ready for bed at night, or take your medicine.

That was before they got the chemistry right. But now you join the other ladies. Herded with them into lunch and exercise and little games and toe-nail time. You had pink fingernails the other day. God help you, they got the medicine right. Like as not, I thought, they'll get you to church.

"She's an atheist," I told them once.

They broke into peals of laughter. I hoped at least they'd take you to a church where there was singing. You'd like the singing, I told myself. You sang in churches when you were young. That was before the opera discovered you.

I found you one morning coming out of the chapel with all the ladies. You'd loved the service. As if something fell into place for you there. As if you were a child again, back with the people who took you to church long ago. Maybe God will forgive you for being an atheist once, now that you're a child again and he can cope with you. You were a believer once. In God, you thought. But no, it was not the church but the choir, not God but the voices that praised him. They need you in the chorus here. You know the songs. You're the only one who knows them all, or can carry a tune.

We hear the opera together today. Arias, on the little CD player I brought. You listen, your head on your pillow, your eyes closed, your hands clenched around mine, singing along with your heroines, Moffo, Te Kanawa, Sills, celebrating the notes you still can reach.

"I used to sing that one," you tell me;
"I know. I heard you sing it."

And now I can hear it again, the sound of your voice years ago. I hear you at your recitals, and at breakfast, and at windows as you water your plants, and in the passenger seat of the car. I see you panicking over a cough an hour before you go on.

Neither the patience nor the drive to be a great diva, but god knows, the voice.

I hear you as Santuzza, Mimi, Manon. I hear the Last Songs and Aida and Cavalleria.
I even hear your fifth-graders doing Peter Pan.

You're sitting by the aquarium, poking at goldfish to get them to dance.

At the lake years ago, out on the dock, a ballet of sunfish would play at your feet, you choreographing the dance with toes and crackers. You celebrated the herons and wild geese and swallows, you lured the raccoons and the possums up to the door.

A feeder for the raccoon: you'd never had a raccoon of your own. We fed her. The next night she brought her babies. They plundered the bird-feeders, emptied the trash, scattered the contents over the yard, sent the barrels tumbling down to the road. Soon you had all the raccoons you could want.

The night the bear came up on the deck, you fell in love. You danced in your heart with the bear. We sat together and watched as he took hold of the bird feeder, got his tongue into the openings, sucked some seeds out. He lumbered over the deck on all fours, walking craters into the snow.
"Lord," you said, "He's gorgeous."
I wouldn't let you throw him an apple. You pouted.

"Kitty kitty," you called to the king of lions, that afternoon at the zoo, and he turned his head and looked straight into your eyes. You'd have reached out and touched him but for the iron bars. You'd have run your fingers through his fur and spoken softly to him. You'd have loved it, so would he.

You cried for a bird striking the window, lamented a roadside woodchuck, mourned a shattered butterfly-wing, you bled for limbs split, blossoms torn, and trees dismembered; you used to hurt for all the broken under heaven.

But the cats, they were your favorites. The ones you invited or tricked or cajoled into coming inside: wild things who arrived at our door, and learned to sit by your side and sprawl over sofas, and lurk in your jungles of potted geranium, spider-plant, ginger.

There was Chaos and Nefertiti and Mr. Moon. There was Clara, who found you wherever you went, and Count Dracula, who serenaded you at an upstairs window till you adopted him. Anyway that's how you told it.

There are photos here of you with the big orange tom. Here's one of him on your shoulder, the way he and you spent a lot of your time together.

You coddled stray invalids; one of your rescues you caressed all the way to the dark when her time had come, and closed her eyes and took her home and dug a hole with your fingers under a pine in the yard and marked the place with a stone.

You used to ask me, "Will you keep my kitties when I'm gone?"

They're with me now. A little bit of you in every one of them: a name you gave it or a vision of it in your lap, or a melody you sang to that one cat and no one else.

One or two of them sleep near me now and slip into my dreams, where I go on looking for something of you I can keep.

You never mention the cats anymore. You only love what's in front of you now, and there are no cats where you are. Now and then somebody brings a dog to Memory House. Now you love dogs.

And you never mention our grownup children:
"Mandy's coming tomorrow," I'd say.
"Mandy who?"
"Our daughter Mandy."
"I don't know her."
"Yes you do. You carried her. She's your baby."
"No, I don't remember her."
"You'll know her when you see her."

"I don't think so."

But she comes, and when she's there in front of you, you love her again.

But you almost remember our house in the hills west of Albany.
"Can't we go there?" you ask me.
"No."
"Then stay with me here."
"I can't. They won't let me."
"You don't like me anymore, you don't want to be with me."
"Yes I do. That's why I come."
"You still do? Really-really?"
"Really-really."
"Why won't you live with me then? I'll make them give me a bigger bed."

Your plants you don't remember at all. Time was, you filled our house with them: delicate waifs and monsters and every size and shape in between. Something in your hands knew what a leaf knows in its veins. There were snake plants and spider plants, ginger, geranium, cacti, euphorbia, violets, hibiscus. I can't remember the rest.

We carried them every fall to the school where you taught, and brought them every summer back home.

Your plants are with Mandy now. She's taking good care of them. The ginger are gone, pretty much, but the orchids and the spider plant and the euphorbia and geraniums are doing pretty well, I hear.

There's a piano at Memory House. You played the other day. But your hands hurt and the keys didn't fit your fingers, and someone had written the notes all wrong.

No plant or piano remembers your hands.

Middle of nights, here in the house we used to share, I still hear you calling my name. In my dreams you still know my name.

You come onstage in one of my dreams. You come as yourself, then you turn into a tiny red bird. You hover over the crowd. You alight here and there on a finger. Then you fly again. You climb higher and higher. You're further and further away, but you never quite disappear.

At first, it had been just lapses of memory. Slowly your dreams seeped into the spaces where your life used to be. Spaces like empty schoolbuses filled up with phantom children, riding to you to learn how to sing. There finally wasn't a time or a place that was safe from your dreams.

"It's like I'm floating above myself most of the time," you told me once. "You're my anchor," you said.

You want me to live in your dreams, among the phantom children. Once, when we started to walk together, you told me one of the children was waiting. You wanted me to go back and find him. I went, I pretended to look.
"Nobody's there. He must have gone home."
"All right. I hope he's okay."

"You've already lost her," somebody said.
"I know."

But it isn't that easy.

"I'm surprised it's you," you told me once, when I came. "I was waiting for the other man."

What other man?

Probably, I thought, it was one of your phantoms. But maybe it was a boyfriend you found in the Home. I tried to picture, among the doddering, one that would do. If one was there, I said to myself, you'd have found him by now. That wasn't fair, but it's what ran through my head.

I stopped myself.
"I'm jealous! Christ almighty, I'm jealous!"
Of maybe nobody. And I thought, What a hold you still have on an old man who's already lost you.

"Do you still love me?" you ask me sometimes, "Even the way I am?"
"I do."

I'm even learning to love anybody you love, real or unreal. I'm learning to love whoever or whatever makes your wreck of a world bearable.

"You've lost her," more than one person has said. "Do your grieving now. It will make things easier."
If I had any sense, that's what I'd do.

But whenever I start to get sensible, I hear the music again, and I feel your hands around mine as we listen.

You sing, and you still know the melodies, and sometimes your high notes go almost where they belong, and you lean into my arms sometimes, and you reach across the music sometimes, for a kiss.

"Vissi d'arte," Te Kanawa sings, "Vissi d'amore."

And you're singing it with her.

And I'll grieve when the music ends.

2

"My grandmother loved me," you told me once long ago. "And my Aunt Dorothy. God knows Dorothy loved me. I never knew whether my mother did, and I hardly ever heard a word from my father. Anyway I was a nuisance. My mother used to set me out on the porch in the morning. I was, I don't know, maybe three or four. And I'd trundle round the corner to my grandma's house, to Gammy's house. And Mama would be free to clean the house and play piano and do whatever else she wanted without me underfoot.

"Gammy and Dorothy were my salvation. I went everywhere with Gammy. She would introduce me as her daughter. She was determined to make a Catholic of me. You know how Catholics are. My Mama was Episcopalian, so I was Episcopalian. Even if we never went to church."

"By the time I was six, I knew what I wanted in life: I wanted wings. I did, I wanted wings. And I had a plan. I would be a saint. I promised Jesus I would pray and go to church and take communion and be nice to everyone. So I could get my wings.
"I remember telling Jesus how good to them I'd be. No one ever fussed over wings the way I would. I'd keep them clean and fluff them out and preen them every night.
"I could just picture them: They'd be dazzling white, with just a touch of gold at the tips, and a glow of pink along the borders.

Then the girl from up the street called me a dummy. She was seven, she knew all about such things. She told me, 'saints ain't got wings, only angels got wings, saints just got a halo.'
"I was crushed. All these months of being good, and all there was to have was a halo."
"Well, I thought at first maybe I'd get one of those and let it go at that."
"Not you," I said. "You wouldn't settle."
"No," You said, "I wouldn't settle. Jesus couldn't put me off that easy."

You finally found a way to soar. You were no saint and no angel. You were a singer.

"I want to make them cry," you told me once. "That's what I want." That's what the music was about: get them sobbing with Manon, make them heartbroken with Butterfly.

Meanwhile, at school, A's fell to you like rain, the music and the history and literature were almost too easy. Even the math: the answers flew into your head. Other kids were struggling with the formulas and getting it right sometimes, but you just knew what the answers were. Finally somewhere in high school, the math got intricate. Math turned on you, and you lost interest in it. There were better things to study anyway.

You were top of your class at Saint Rose, a little Catholic College in Albany.
"I was a terror," you told me "I was always shocking the nuns. Or they pretended to be shocked. I think they got a kick out of it, some of them. And some of them were always trying to save me. You know how nuns are. But I guess some of them only thought I was a spoiled little protestant snot."
You paused and looked at me, as if to give me time to say you weren't spoiled. I didn't say anything.

"And probably I was," you finally said. "One of them prayed for me. I was such a gifted girl, she told me. She couldn't bear to see my soul go to waste."

"I don't know what possessed me to marry the guy," you told me of a first husband. Then you admitted, "Yes I do. I know. We were young and crazy. And he was wild, and he was fun. But god, if I'd known what was coming…"

"We had been married for eight or nine years," you said, "when I got the clot in my lungs. On my back in a hospital bed, for I don't know how long. Seemed like forever. Didn't dare move. Everybody thought sure as hell I was a goner."

"Dying ruined my marriage," you told me. "I came home and started throwing stuff out. Started getting rid of things I used to think I needed. I'd especially had enough of him.

When I came the first time to your house, to take you to dinner, there were three of you there: you and your daughter Mandy (seven years old), and Underfoot, your big unaltered scruffy tom. I fell in love with all three of you.

Anyway, you and I went to dinner: a little French restaurant in Albany, one of the few places you would later remember even after you'd forgotten nearly everything else. And we went on seeing each other. Sometimes you and I and Mandy and the cat had dinner at your house.

You frowned one night at the paper clip I used, to hold a bachelor sleeve together. With a straight face I said: "I Couldn't find a safety pin". You sighed and sewed a button on. "Why don't you let anyone do things for you?" you said, "Why don't you?" I don't recall ever seeing you sew a button on anything since.

I remember Mandy on the sofa next to me, arm locked vice-like round my elbow, her eyes two big silly marbles green-lighting the stalled traffic that my life was in those days.

"We could have our dinners here, the three of us," you said at one point.
"That would be nice…you mean all the time? Every night?"
"You could call me when you couldn't come."
"Oh."
"Tell me what you think."
Like an idiot I did.
"You don't appreciate me," you said. "Why should I waste my youth on you? Maybe I'll find someone else, now I'm over hating men. Maybe you'll regret you did that for me."

But I recall going home that night, and scanning the bachelor mess I lived in: beer-cans scattered on the floor, torn dusty paper drapes, and stuff piled up at random everywhere. "How could anybody live here?" you had asked. Now that I knew you, nobody did.

The weekend in Rhode Island, just you and me, the putting a few days together, that much risk and promise. We drove across Massachusetts and down the coast, to beaches, boats, and tide rocks, then the last room in the last motel in town.

Out in the foggy morning to the lighthouse at Point Judith. You running, standing in the spray at Moonstone beach. I sitting on a log and waiting for you. You gathered what you said were moonstones, and a mussel shell.

But the real turning point came one night at your house. I had said something inexcusable, which I had a way of doing in those days, mostly without realizing it.

Can't remember what it was: I only know it was inexcusable because you cried, and Mandy ran away upstairs. I stood there in shock, more amazed than penitent: I'd never dared imagine anyone was mine to hurt. From that moment on, nothing was the same. I leafed back through my life, looking for the old familiar emptiness. I couldn't find it.

I proposed to you in a parking lot, while we were waiting for traffic to clear, so we could back out and go home. It was a concert at Saratoga. I'd been thinking about it all week and I just blurted it out: "Marry me". You said, "Okay."

I met your family: a tribal dinner. Talked of fishing with your father, of children with your mother and your aunt, heard folk-remedies for tooth-ache from your grandma. Then the young came dancing through the room and shouting, while the dog sat in her corner stareddy-eyed at me. Your mother initiated me with a camera. She looked at you and sighed and shook her head and dubbed me "More-guts-than-brains", and I had a clan identity.

You needed a church wedding. You were still comfortable in churches in those days. Only a few guests, at a side-altar of a little Episcopal Church in Albany. We observed all the rituals: rings and magical phrases and wedding cake. There was even a November honeymoon in Jamaica.

"I feel like a kid," you said as we left. "I've never been on a real vacation."

I remember a week or so after we got back, there was this big Polish party: your father's side of the family. I begged off. A more or less legitimate cold.

"It was wild," you said, arriving back home, "If you could have gone and been invisible, you'd have loved it."

If I could have been invisible. You were right, you were married to a recluse. Would have rather gone to my own life by the back door and not have to play a role in it. Would have liked to know my new in-laws without having to meet too many of them. I wasn't fit company in those days. You never quite civilized me, but you taught me to soften the things I used to say, till they weren't unforgivable, but merely offensive. Or even to shut up sometimes.

We were staying then in the house in Albany where you'd lived, with its roof that leaked and its muddy basement floor, and its tyrannical Wisteria, that clung to the outside walls, smothered the porch, put tendrils all the way to the roof.

My first week there, my new daughter took me on a tour of the yard, pointing out the mock orange and the wild roses. And was there an apple? An elm? I can't recall.

We of course couldn't live there long. Had to find a place for our new life together. And besides there were too many ghosts for you there, it was as if the walls were still infected with lies you'd been told.

When we bought a house in Slingerlands, in the suburbs, you took a few living mementos: a chestnut seedling, house plants, and a cutting of wisteria.

You loved the new house, so much that at first you thought you didn't want ever to leave it.

"I wouldn't have to work, you know: I could stay home."
"What, and be a housewife? And not teach anymore?"
"And be a housewife, yes,"
"You'd be bored to death."
"No, it'd be nice. I never get a chance to keep things up the way I'd like to. I love this house and this yard, never had a place I loved before. I want a garden and I never have any time for it."
"You'll get over it," I said. And of course you did.

Later, when your mother left you the house on a lake in the Helderberg Hills, we began to spend our summers there.

You taught me to sing. You were very patient with me. We did duets from Tosca and Manon Lescaut. For one summer you had me thinking like a tenor. I insulted several Italian arias.

I was in the audience one summer night when you sang something of Puccini. Old guy covering the recital for the local newspaper heard you sing, and he'd seen me with you.
"That your daughter?"
"No. My wife."
"Well, I'll be damned. You're a lucky man, she's fantastic. Helluva voice."
He liked your looks too, I gathered.
"Your wife, huh? How long you been married?"
"Not long."
"You'll have some fun with that one yet."

You told me all about the long-distance phone-call from the old-friend-who-still-loved-you. He'd been full of questions, you said. Might we be moving near him? Did you need a job? Should he call again? He'd be discreet, he said. You said he shouldn't but you thought he might. I fell into the trap and reacted like a fool. I think you wanted jealousy, you needed to get used to being needed.

And God knows you were needed. I was obsessed with you. I stalked you with a pen: "Felt like Scheherezade" you told me once. "Like I had to be forever finding a new episode to keep you interested. And you remember everything. Thank god I haven't told you many lies."

I met Mary your sister, your cousin really but more like a sister (as both of you told everyone). Mary, tough, clever Mary, by your side whenever you needed somebody: when you were stung by a bee, when you needed an advocate in a hospital or needed someone to look after this or that for you, Mary was there.

And I met Dorothy. Dorothy, your mother's spinster sister, your beloved maiden aunt, the family patron saint and sage. "She predicted we'd get married," you confided to me once, a long time later.

Dorothy, as awkward as I was among people. We circled each other, Dorothy and I, when I first met her. Like two shy animals who'd found at one time the same water-hole.
"You were both looking for somewhere to hide," you told me later. "When you both realized that, you were okay."

"It's incurable, what I have," Dorothy told me that day, "but they can control it."

You told me later: It was her kidneys, slowly being eaten away by Lupus, one of the family curses.

"Saturdays used to be Dorothy days at our house," you told me. "She played games with the kids. They cheated at cards to make her laugh. They'd hide a glove or steal an overshoe when she was about to leave."

The kids, you said. The kids, plural: there was a son here once, I had learned, before he went off to live with his father.

You told me all about the kids.

Mandy, you told me, had ventured bald and bug-eyed out of you one April, and for the longest time hardly made a sound. It worried you, how still she was. when it was time to be talking. She never spoke a word, until one weekend when she had it all together: then she blossomed into dialogue and prophesy, and hasn't shut up since. Hasn't stopped advising you on everything from diet and the kind of catfood you are buying to the way you do your hair and wear your life.
Your son was a stranger case. "Matt spent his first few days just being saved," you said. "Nobody thought he'd live. He was a mess. Only one eye worked, and one ear, and one hand was deformed and one leg. Doctors somehow got him through. Anyway while they were saving him, he and I were apart; he and I never had any mother-and-baby stuff, any touching or warmth. By the time we got together he felt like a stranger."

Matt still lived with his father when Dorothy died, and you wanted your son back: you wanted to rescue him.
"I yearn for him," you said, but you admitted: "My redemption isn't going to be easy on any of us."

Anyway we brought him home. And you were right, it wasn't easy. There was the fat lip he gave his sister the first week.
"We used to be so happy," Mandy said through the hurt.

A solid house was suddenly fragile with loud footfalls and shouts and an occasional threat. We loved him out of desperation: nothing else to do with him, not enough room in the house to let somebody rattle around loose and unloved.

I taught him chess. He was a terror at tactics.

You taught him the piano. He had talent. If only he'd had two hands that worked.

He was a god-awful pest in your garden. He was your self-appointed weed. He'd screw up something and you'd scold him, and he'd flower you a devilish smile. Rather be damned for a terrorist than a clod. But he couldn't stay out of your garden any more than the dandelions could.

Maybe we'd have done better with Matt if we had been gentler and wiser and better at caring for someone who didn't dare be cared for.

When the time came, You gathered up a grandson too. Found him huddled in his room while Matt and his wife, his mom and dad, were screaming at each other. He would sit at his computer, he would squeeze into the hard-drive, he would run away among the figures in a game while his dad and mama's house came crashing down. We took him in, for that one year.

3

Larry keeps breaking things (you said of me, in the last year of your journal.) He never can see things in front of his face. I think he's going downhill.

Cellar flooding. Must be spring.
Forgot to call Mandy on her birthday.
Can't get through to my grandson or his poor mother. She thinks it's all right if Alex fails a course or two.

Larry said we could keep Alex this year. I'm glad he said it. I was so torn. I wanted to keep him but I knew Larry feels too old for that sort of thing.

All the cats have been getting out. Door isn't closing right. Tubby's the cleverest at wedging it open. But they all come back.

Great weather for Alison's outdoor wedding. Best wedding I've ever been to. Wonderful food and drinks. Geese flew over and pooped on the congregation. And the band was spectacular. There was a chorus line of bridesmaids and a best man and a best dog. Filet mignon to die for.

Alex has come. Got him started on homework. He's staying up late on his computer, but I don't mind as long as he does his homework first.

Went swimming. Weeds are back. Curly pond weed. Water-lilies are all over the lake and smell wonderful. Deerflies and mosquitoes are teeming. Wisteria is a disaster at Slingerlands. You can't get through it and I'm too tired to do outside work.

Alex wiggling out of whatever he can. Plays computer games all night. Can't stay awake in school. Mandy came. Did lots of work. Shutters upstairs. Cellar neatened.

Larry got the wrong vodka (of course.) I guess it's the medicine that makes me so picky.

Raccoon stole the water dish, and Motley's bed, and the feeder. He poops on the porch. Mandy has lots of new goats and beautiful chickens that lay colored eggs.

Mary came to help us catch Dolf. To go to the vet. He ran into a closet, then he ran downstairs. Larry and Mary had him in a blanket but as we put him in a cage he escaped and bit me in the ankle. Very deep. Went to ER.

Alex is slacking on his homework.

Pain is so bad I do nothing but sit and hurt and wait for the next pill. Robbie is missing.

Coyotes very close to the house last night. Made my hair stand on end. Couldn't get back to sleep.

Alex in a midnight homework marathon. Marking period ends tomorrow at noon. He'll never finish in time.

So sick of picking up everything Larry started and didn't finish. It's always half-assed and I know he does a lot but I am getting so tired and sick.

Larry picked up Alex at school. I'm not so sure I like Alex riding with him. He's such a rotten driver.

Beautiful day. Went walking. It made my back hurt. Sat on the deck with Larry for awhile.

Creamsickle hasn't come home. I'm heartsick. He's been gone since yesterday afternoon. I walked up and down the road, calling Kitty. He'd be home to eat if he could.

Alex's report card was terrible. Matt won't do anything about it.

Larry and I getting tense over my operation tomorrow. Nervous about the operation. Want to do it. Wish it was over. (Anyway, Creamsickle's back.)

Awful in the hospital. Kept thinking I was somewhere else. It was scary. Had to fight to get a nurse to come. As usual everything was screwed up.

I have been playing a lot of Grieg but pain is limiting me to 15 minutes before I can't stand it. The pain goes sometimes but not for long. But Buttons keeps me going. When I'm really down he comes and sits with me and purrs and purrs and purrs. Don't know what I'd do without him.

Conference at school. Told them what Alex has been through. They felt he was depressed and very angry, but that he was improving. I liked them but I don't think any of them are good at what they do. (Maybe one exception). And his counselor is worthless.

Larry got the steam-mop but wouldn't help clean. Claimed he couldn't figure it out. College professor can't understand a steam-mop.

Alex got suspended from school for hacking into the faculty computer. He insists on going back to his mama, I think because I wouldn't let him on the computer till he did his homework.

It's evening already; feels like I only woke a minute ago. I don't remember a thing that happened today.

Larry's having a fit about Motley. She got in but is being good so far. Can't see why Larry is so upset. So she peed on his pillow. We can always buy another pillow.

The birds are back; I love the birds, can't recall the name of a single one.

Bear on the deck three nights in a row. Shattered the gate, but used the same one every time he came, so he didn't break anything more. Very thoughtful bear.

Robbie is missing. Hopefully will be back tomorrow.
I wanted to send cards today. Can't think of anyone's name. I think some bastard shot the bear.

Can never say what I want to say: the words don't come. Anyway I told Larry how I felt about his not being at all interested doing anything pertaining to the house. Bad idea.

Finally Wee Robbie came home. I've been so worried. He seems healthy but feral again. I'm not letting him out.

Thought I wrote in this book yesterday: it was a month ago.

Larry trying to help more. I feel like Larry and Mary think I'm an idiot. I'm not, I keep telling myself, just terribly forgetful.

Robbie is missing again.

There the journal entries stopped.

4

I'm looking out at the snow, up here at the lake, remembering winters we spent together.

One January it snowed two feet and then froze and then snowed some more. The weight of the ice and the wind brought more than one tree down over the power lines and they barely missed the house. We were adrift in outage, I dashing here and there after flashlights and not finding any, trying and failing to get through to the power company on the phone. You meanwhile assembling candles, going out for firewood. We stayed the first night in the chill and huddled around the fireplace. But the birch wood was too freshly cut. It made a slow and smoky flame and we ran out of kindling. And the house turned colder and dark and you cried a long time in my arms before we made our escape.

And one chilly May morning we ran outside together to shake the new snow off the lilacs. Our lilacs lined one whole wall of the house and stretched up the bricks to the second floor and reached around the corner of the house and spilled over onto the deck. I remember you tugging at branches while the snow fell over your hair and your shoulders.

There was our drunken hell-bent ride together in one winter storm, coming home from I-don't-remember-where: some fool party I think. I peering through the last un-iced square inch or two of windshield. We celebrated the crazy way up the hill and home, you laughing at the craziness of it and at the way I drove.
"If I hadn't been a drunk you never would have married me," I said, "I'd have been too dull for you."
"Probably," you said.

And once, on the clearest and coldest of nights, you called me: "Come look at the stars!" We stepped out into the yard together. You hurried ahead, and I stood at the brink of the dark, tottering with my terrible balance. And you came back for me, and steadied me. And together we celebrated the stars in the clearest brightest night-sky of the year.

And one February not so long ago, this big storm stalled on the coast, and brought half the Atlantic back over us. God shoveled a whole winter down on us in a week. We were too old for this. Weather-guy on T V had no mercy, showing us houses with roofs caved in, as five feet of snow piled up over us. Meanwhile, across the road in the woods, the giants kept crashing down under the weight. We were almost surprised that year that the sun came back and then the rain came, and the white washed away.

When you retired, you still taught piano, and gave now and then a singing lesson, but there were no classrooms full of kids. There were no musical games to teach them, no concerts or musical comedies to rehearse. And you sank into a god-awful funk, that wouldn't end till you found someone to take their place. The cats.

A cat like a kid was someone to fret over. A cat was someone to scold for digging up the soil of the giant ginger, someone to comfort you, climbing onto your bed or your lap, pressing a face against your face, or touching you with a forepaw, softly or with a few urgent prickles extended.

You had loved pedigreed cats: you bought an Abyssinian. At a cat-show, you rescued a silver tabby who'd just ended his showbiz career (you said) by biting a judge. But then up at the lake, people started dropping off their unwanted cats. And you rescued them. Some little corner of the world was yours to save again.

And you saved more and more of them, till savages ran wild and lurked around every corner and padded silent through the house and scalped the furniture. Cat-hairs scattered everywhere like arrows.

Cats would gather at sunup and surround us in bed.
"Don't chase them away," you'd tell me.
The bed would be crowded half an hour later.

Years later, when you had come to Memory House, they wouldn't let you have a cat. But you almost believed in the big plush toy tiger I got you for Christmas. Sometimes you knew he wasn't real but you told me he loved you anyway and he knew you loved him. And he had the heart of the big orange tom they wouldn't let you bring to The House. You stroked his fur, you kissed him. You hugged him close to you. And when you crossed the room, his strange eyes followed you. His paws settled into your hands sometimes and the shape of him fit your memory of the big orange tom. And he sat on your lap when you put him there. And he rode with you up and down the hall on your walker.

5

"Oh god, I hurt," you said, one night at the house on the lake. It was worse, it was very much worse. Pills for the pain were no help that night. I was dialing the phone.

"Who are you calling?" you said.
"Who do you think?"
"I won't go to a hospital. I'd rather die here."
"You're not going to die."
"You talk like you don't know how sick I am."
"I know…"
"No you don't. I wish you could feel for an hour what this is."
"Come on, let's go."
"No. Please just stay and hold my hand."
"Come on for Christ's sake."
"What can they do for me? What's the point? What did they do last time? I don't want to die in a hospital. I want you to hold my hand, that's all."
"I'll hold your hand when we get there," I said.
"Who are we kidding? You know I'm dying."
"I don't know any such…"
"People know when they're going to die."

I couldn't think of a come-back.

One of the cats came into your lap, and put his head next to yours. You stroked it.
"He knows what I need," you said. Then your tone hardened:
"Listen, you don't have to stay with me. Sleep downstairs if you like. That way you won't have to wake up beside a dead body."
"Oh for the love of…"
"I said I won't go and I meant it."
"I'd like to pick you up and drag you there."
"I know."

I thought of a drastic compromise.
"If in the morning you're not dead yet, will you go?"

And you laughed and said yes.
And in the morning, you were not dead. You tried to renege.
I wouldn't let you: "You promised."
You nodded but held out again: "What for?"

"For me. For the cats. We're selfish. We can't live without you."
"You're crazy."
"I know. Come on."

And you laughed. Then you cried.
And we went.

A day of waiting in the ER, a day of hurting and of questions and of tests, of falling off to fitful sleep, then waking and complaining that you couldn't sleep, then falling off to sleep again.

Can we get a pill for pain?
A bedpan. Can we get a bedpan? Nurse? Is there a nurse here somewhere?
Finally they got you a room.

Middle of the night, you woke:

"Am I dead?"
"What?"
"Am I dead?"
"It's okay. Everything's okay."
"I'm not alive. I don't feel alive. Nothing's real. Why is nothing real?"
"I don't know what you mean."
"It's not a real place, it's not a real room."
"Sure it is. What is it then?"
"The doors and windows are just painted on. It's like a set. A theater set. We're in a play. It isn't the real world."
"Yes it is."
"No. And what are you doing here? Are you dead too?"
"Nobody's dead."
When I looked at you again, you were asleep.

When you woke again, you said, "Where are we?"
"In a hospital," I said.
"What am I doing here?"
"It's okay, we just have to wait awhile"
"What are we waiting for?"
"The doctor is coming."
"I want to go home."
"Not yet, we have to wait for the doctor."
"How long?"
"It takes awhile, they have other patients."
"I'm going, where are my clothes?"
"It isn't time yet."
"Find me my clothes."
"I can't."
"Get out of my way, I'm going home."
"Like that? In a hospital gown?"

"There's my coat. I'm going."
"How are you going to get there?"
"Don't you have a car? Won't you take me?"
"No, I can't."
"Why not? You don't care about me."
"I do."
"If you don't take me right now, I won't ever speak to you again."
"We have to wait for the doctor."
You tore the IV out of your arm, put your coat on over your hospital gown and trudged in your hospital socks toward the exit. They had to give you something to quiet you.

Two doctors entered your room at the end of the day.

"Does she have a DNR?"
"Does she have a what?
"A DNR. Do not resuscitate."
"Oh."
Does she have one?
"I don't think so."

Omigod. Was it that bad?

6

"Take me to see my mother," you'd say.
Then you'd admit, "I don't even know where she is."
Then softly, "But she's not there anymore, is she?"
"No."
"She's gone, isn't she?"
A few minutes later you couldn't forgive her for never coming to see you.

Nouns escaped you. Thank god for colors.
"Look at the green." "What is that black?" "Can I have some of the red?"
Books were impossible: by the time chapter two had come, chapter one was gone.
Everything had to be won again tomorrow from the beginning.

I walked in the front door one day and you told me, "Your brother called."
"Who?" I said.
"Your brother. On the telephone."
"I have a sister," I reminded you, "I don't have a brother"
You didn't answer.
But a day or two later you told me he had come by, my brother had come to the house. You had let him in. You'd talked, the two of you. And you looked into my eyes and didn't know which brother I was.

Later you found several of me, all of us declaring we'd married you many years ago. You asked one morning which of us had just slept with you. For a minute you saw how weird that was.
"Make sense of this for me," you said. And God knows I wanted to.

"She's coming to take me," you told me once, "I have to get ready."
"Who's coming?"
"I can't recall who."
"To take you to what?"
"I don't know. What if she doesn't come? I can't get there by myself."
"Get where?"
"I told you, I don't know where."
"Then why do you have to go?"
"They're waiting for me."
"Who's waiting?"
"Stop it. Will you please stop it?"

There were choruses at night through the walls. I tried to hear them with you. Discordant voices, you said. I listened for them. A horrible music, you said, a threatening music. And that I couldn't hear it with you made it worse. Other things you saw or heard I could not see or hear. It was then you began to distrust me.

I wanted to keep you with me. "I'd rather share the nightmare with her," I told somebody, "than make her face it alone." As if a nightmare were something to share. The nightmares, yours and mine, were separate. There came a point where one house could not hold both of them.

7

Hi Mandy

It did your mother a lot of good, your spending the day with her. Thank God you were here when she made the dash for the lake. She simply refuses to let anything put her off. Once she decides she wants to do something you'd have to tackle her to prevent it. She's promised not to do that again. But of course she won't remember the promise.

Been frantic here since the last e-mail. We were back in the hospital on Wednesday. Your mother fell over the bed and gashed her leg. I'll let you know tomorrow how we're doing.

Your mama seems all right this morning. She can't remember being in the hospital. But she seems tired. Meanwhile, she is, as of today, totally refusing to take any pills at all (on principle, no less).

She is two persons. One of them knows me and loves me and knows I love her. The other (and there's no telling when it will emerge) remembers only that the house on the lake belongs to her (her mother left it to her) and she doesn't know who I am. Therefore I am an intruder.

Your mother frantic last night: no kitties had come to bed with her. Then she found some of them with me. She decided I must have stolen them and demanded that I give them back and then leave and never return. When I didn't go, she asked me to call the police for her (she couldn't find the number) so that I could be physically expelled from the house. After some medicine-laced ice cream, your mother went quietly to bed, and in the morning, aside from a little more grogginess than usual, was her old self. We have just had lunch and she's resting quietly now.

Today she wanted me out of the house because her imaginary friends were coming, and she thinks they're afraid of me (which I think she concludes from the fact that I've never seen a single one of them.)

Saw Dr. Pica Tuesday. New med list. Trimmed down to the essentials. Not much different from what I had ended up doing anyway. Getting 4 or 5 pills a day at best. Some of her imaginary friends turn out to be medical geniuses, who are advising against Pica's recommendations.

Your mother has suddenly started insisting again that I'm an intruder in the house and telling me to get out or she'll call the police. This goes on all day sometimes.

We're on our way to St. Peters. She took a fall and is yelling at me t0 get the hell out of her life forever while the ambulance comes. I'll call you from the hospital.

Your mother surpassed all previous records at the hospital. She got uncontrollable. St. Peters gave up on her, declared her healthy and threw us out.

We got home late last night. She was lovely until the effects of the lortab wore off.

Finally got a prednosone into her at 1:30 am. She woke very sick. We've done a little better on the pills today.

This time your mother has succeeded in getting the police on the phone. She needed me, the intruder, to give them the address.

Cops showed up, three of them, in two squad cars. One of them explained to your mother patiently that there was nothing they could do because this is my legal residence.

She told him it IS NOT and informed the lot of them that they were useless.

Suddenly for no apparent reason, things are better. She loves me again. Pica has come up with a new med, which I still have to retrieve at the pharmacy. I'll keep in touch.

No police so far today. Today your mother had a good idea. She thinks she and I should get married. I told her we're already married. She laughed and said no.

I'm finally admitting to myself I'm over my head. She found her keys the other day and drove the truck up and down the road, she keeps threatening to swim across the lake. I can't keep her out of danger, and she won't take her pills. And I'm going out of my mind.

Thanks for the info on adult homes. I've been getting some recommendations. Will you come with me this week and look at some places?

Our last year together at the lake, you threw yourself at your life the way you always had, but without judgment, with nothing to slow you down or break your fall.

I remember telling Mary once that I'd never send you away to one of those places where old people go to die. But I sent you to one of those places, didn't I.

We hustled you into the car that summer, and drove you to Memory House. You were okay with it. You even enjoyed the ride, I think. You sat patiently and waited while we met with the people at Memory House. We stayed there a little while with you. You started to come with us as we went toward the door. What did we mean, "Goodbye"?

"I'm coming back," I said. A coward, I didn't add, "It won't be today."

8

You very soon got used to Memory House: soon "Get me out of here" turned into "come and stay with me."
"I want us to be together." you'd say.
I'd put you off: "We're together now."
"I know you don't want to be with me."
"I do. I like to be with you. That's why I come."
"You like the other ladies"
"You're my only one." (which so help me god was true, is true.)
"Really?"
"Really."
"Then why don't you stay with me?"
"I come to see you all the time."
"But you don't stay."
"I stay a long while."
"I want you to stay all night."
"I can't."
"Why not?"
"Because they don't do things that way here."
"Then let's go somewhere else."

Once you were settled at Memory House, we'd sit together for hours in your room, and you'd tell me stories. Now, when you were saying only a few-words-at-a-time you were fine. So long as there were no nouns, you made sense. But sentences with more than eight or ten words, or full of words that were easy to forget, were too much: you slipped into nonsense, especially the stories you told, and sometimes you couldn't stop telling them:

"And so he said well that isn't more like a corner to come by again without hitting someone on the head, and somebody said she can do it better than anybody and I did and they did it too then and we all laughed."
I said, "I see."
You went on. "And we came off in another one more than the little black circles but we knew there had to be a lot more on top of another one but you're not supposed to find this and run all over and tell people and they wanted to make the doing one and I couldn't and he liked it but he doesn't want to go out and fall down over it."
"Oh," I said, "I didn't know that."
"So we went because they knew there weren't any going off that way today because of her getting all scratched like that in the middle and we didn't have any torny ones especially in green…"
"Hmmm," I said.
"Am I driving you nuts?" you suddenly asked.
"No. no." I said, taken aback. I was always startled when you came back into the comprehensible.
"You looked like I was driving you nuts."
"No, everything's okay."
"I didn't make you mad, did I?"
"You never make me mad."
"Do you still like me?"
"Yes, I still like you."

You smiled and went on with your story:
"Anyway we tried, and she got there without breaking it and the black little ball the shape of a hotsy totsy came and just as you thought everyone might they went away off in another one but not very long because there wasn't much to fly there."

You paused. "Do you love me even now that I'm a cuckoo?"
"You're not any such…"
"Yes I am. I know I am. Do you still love me anyhow?"
"I will always love you."
"Really-really?"
"Really-really."

One Sunday when Mandy and I were there to see you, Mary came too, and your face lit up. It was a family gathering. Like the old days. You were thrilled. You always so loved family gatherings.

At Memory House, sometimes you loved everybody. And you let everybody know. Round the dinner table, pointing at one of the ladies and then another, "I love *you* and I love *you* and I love *you*." It never seemed to bother you that no one answered.

It occurred to me that the last phrase ever to cross your lips would probably be "I love you."

You loved some of the attendants and not others. Your favorites you allowed to give you pills, and help you with your clothes and shower. And of course you told them that you loved them. Others were not smiling when they tried to make you take your medicine. You did not forgive them.

"They take things," you said. "They come in and they take my things."
"Take what?" I asked. "Clothes?"
"Uh-huh."
"They take them and wash them," I said. "Then they bring them back."
"No they don't."
"They do. When they bring them back, they're clean."
"I never see them do that," you said.
"I have. I've seen them bring them in and put them away."
"I don't think so."
"Are you getting hungry?" I changed the subject.
"Yes," you said. "I haven't eaten in three days."
"Don't they give you breakfast? I bet you had breakfast."
"No."
"Well, they'll have lunch in twenty minutes."
"No they won't. They say they will but they never do."
"They will."
"Where? Where do they do that?"
"In the dining room."
"Where's that?"
"Right up the hall. That way."
"Really?"
"Sure."
"I've never been there. Will you show me where…"
"I'll go with you."
"Oh will you?"
"We'll go together."
"Can we go now?"
"In twenty minutes."
"Why can't we go now?"
"They're still fixing it."
"Tell me when it's time?"
"I will."
"Will you come with me?"

"Yes I will."
"Oh good. I love you."

Most days, by mid-afternoon the stuff they gave you at the House, to quiet your pain and your fear, started wearing off, the fog cleared a little. Suspicion and hurting and terror would start closing in on you. Your morning playmates disappeared, and villains slipped in through cracks in the wood and waited around corners. Even the shapes you trusted in mornings turned sinister, and stared at you together and conspired. Mid-afternoon was the worst.

I'd try to imagine what it was like to be you. Nothing was real and everything was: whatever you knew you'd half-invented and five minutes later forgotten. Moments would weave themselves and come undone in one motion. "Thank god it was only a dream" was nothing you'd say anymore. Nothing was only-a-dream. Then I'd admit to myself I had no idea what it was like to be you.

When the pain was worst, you'd tell me, "I'm dying" and trace your pain across your fingers to your palms and up your forearms to your shoulders.
"Someone did it to me," you'd tell me; "he did it on purpose."
"It's the arthritis." I'd tell you.
"No it isn't.
"It is. That's what the doctor said."
"I don't have a doctor."

We spent more and more time listening to operatic arias on CD's.
"I used to do these," you would say as you'd said many times before.
"I know. I heard you do them."
"Did you?"
"Yes I did. Lots of times."
"I was good."

"Yes you were."
"I used to be smart," you said.
"Top of your class at college," I said.
"Yes, I was."
"You're still pretty smart."
"No, I'm not. I know I'm not."
We'd be listening, and sometimes you'd say something like
"Oh God, she's good. Who is that?"
And I'd tell you and you'd know who she was. Sometimes just for a minute you'd be who-you'd-been.

But there have been times when being with you was hard. One day in particular last summer. Felt like I had to escape. But you were afraid. I should have stayed. I should have forgotten the things I imagined I had to do, and stayed. They'd look after you here, I told myself. And I'm sure they did. But you were afraid. And as usual, you didn't know quite where you were or quite what to do. You didn't know where the dining room was.

I got you sitting down at lunch and one of the other ladies was sitting beside you, and somebody came with the pill for your pain. And they'd brought the fruit and they'd brought the soup. Can't be with you all the time, I told myself. But you were afraid. And I left you. And I'm sorry.

You were forever sliding your wedding band on and off, there at Memory House, and setting it down here or there. It would get discovered on floors, in a drawer, on the rug under your bed. Almost exactly a year after you came to The House, you lost it one more time. No one has found it since.

And finally the Other Man had a face and a name; this time the boyfriend was real and no phantom. He lived with you now in your half-lighted world at Memory House. You told everyone he's your husband. "I have two husbands," you told somebody.

He wasn't one of the doddering males I'd grown used to seeing there at the House. Big fellow, not as old as the others. Didn't look like he belonged there.

He was good to you, and he was *there*, somebody was *with* you, in the long lonely hours of your bewilderment.

And I said to myself as I have so often, "I've already lost you."
"I'm learning to love whom you love," I said once, and I meant it then, and yet…

One morning you asked me, "Do you still love me?"
"You know I do," I said
"Do you love him?"
"What?" (Did I hear you right?)
"Do you love him?"
"I don't know him," I said.

But one day soon after that, the Other Man at Memory House was gone. I never knew what had happened. But people had a way of disappearing at Memory House. And I never asked. It was as if he'd never been there. I honestly think you didn't recall him at all. I'd been ready to be an adult and let you go. But you were ecstatic to see me, you hurried behind your walker to meet me.

"I want you to stay all day and all night but you never do," you told me. "I keep thinking I'll never see you again." (I think you didn't say it that clearly, but I can't remember your exact words and anyway I knew what you meant.)

"You will always see me." I said.
"I love you so much," you told me.
And in the weeks that followed, we grew closer and closer.

And I said to myself, I don't know who we are anymore: a child and a parent, or two old people who live in two separate worlds, or two lost children together, or two old people playing at being two young people in love.

For awhile at Memory House I was still the husband you proudly paraded in front of the other ladies. But the husband was to morph slowly into 'the man who comes to see me sometimes'. A man who would no longer have a name.

9

I sat one morning lately at 5 a m, in the house your mama left you by the lake, writing a letter I'd never send you. You wouldn't have remembered the lake, or that there was a house on it. But I needed to tell you:

The forsythia have come and gone, the first slow green is on the lilac-leaves, the bloom is on the world's tallest pear-tree, in the yard. That's what you used to call it. The geese are back. The tree sparrows have flown. We've had no redpolls here this year. Goldfinches are summer-colored again. Purple finches, red-winged blackbirds, song sparrows all are here. You didn't know their names the last few springs, but you loved to look at them.

There were ducks on the lake, as there are every spring and autumn. Ring-necks and scaups and mergansers. Summer belonged to the Canada Geese. Three or four pairs of them every year, and their young, parading across the surface. Every year we had watched the young geese grow up. And in autumn the great twilight flights of them.

You loved the wild geese. But the geese were a pest to some of the neighbors. They'd bring the goslings up on the lawns to forage, and leave the place cluttered with droppings. That's why the people stretched lengths of clothesline along the shore a few inches off the ground, to keep the geese off. But of course the Mama-geese lifted the lines so the babies could pass underneath.

The man next door managed to fall over one of the lines and sued the Lake Society and won, and the insurance went sky-high and so did the dues. And the man next door placed his shed near the property line so that every year the snow came plummeting off and shattered our fence again. You hated the man next door. When he died this year you were already at Memory House and wouldn't have remembered him. Perfectly good death gone to waste.

You'd been at Memory House for less than a year when the furnace shut off in the empty Slingerlands house in the coldest February on record. And the pipes froze. I didn't get back there till the beginning of March, when opening the door I discovered Niagara rushing out of a massive hole in the kitchen ceiling, flushing debris over the kitchen floor into the basement, splashing over the walls, rushing into the living room, soaking the oriental rug and the sofa, running over the legs of the grand piano. Rubble of plaster and wood everywhere. Fine hardwood floor of the dining room plowed into great furrows. Shelves and cupboards and cabinets warped out of shape, smell of mold everywhere. All the doors swollen with water.

A house you'd fussed over for years, forever adding an elegant touch here and there: overhanging shelves for your collection of antique teapots, the grand piano, the tiles from Holland, the grandfather clock. You always knew exactly where every piece had to go. And my carelessness turned it to rubble. At least, I consoled myself, you'd never see this. You wouldn't remember the house, let alone what was in it, let alone all the years you'd put into it. All the years came tumbling down one winter when an old man failed to keep proper watch.

10

One morning there at The House, you swallowed into your lungs some piece of your lunch till it gathered around it a sinister crew and turned into pneumonia. And nothing they tried at the hospital did any good.

Clutching my arm, you cursed me for not saving you. Screamed at me, "Get me the hell out of here!" Then you shouted, just as loudly and furiously, "I love you!" Over and over again, louder and louder: "I LOVE YOU!"

It was the last thing I remember hearing you say.

But your voice sounded awful. Doctors wanted to put this desperate gadget on you. I said, "Try anything."

A day later, I stood by the bed, and you half-opened your eyes and I think you almost smiled.

Mandy and Mary I met with a lot of doctors and psychologists and god-knows-who-else. A doctor finally said he wanted to "Make her comfortable," By which he meant (and I should have seen it coming) take you off the machine and give you up, and let you go.

And I heard from everyone in the room all the reasons why he was right. Everyone was so logical. "She never would have wanted to live this long the way she is," Mary said. It was true. There was a time when you knew enough to want to die. And if I'd been thinking of you, that's what I would have wanted.

And they waited for me to say it. A roomful of eyes trained on me, waiting. And I knew how selfish it was, but I said, "I can't do this today."

"What's your goal?" the doctor asked, meaning I guess, "What the hell do you want from this poor wretched ruin of a woman?" I didn't have any goals, I just didn't want you to die.

What *did* I want, I asked myself that night: Did I want to watch you go where your friends at the House were going? Inez, good company once, had stopped talking, pretty much. Now she mostly sat there staring straight ahead. Your friend Gerry who used to sit up from time to time and smile and tell you to eat your soup, could hardly hold her head up anymore. Helen needed awakening three or four times every meal. Was that what I wanted for you?

Sitting alone that night in the house, I needed a drink. For the first time in forty years, I needed a drink. Thank god there wasn't one there in the house.

Forty years. My god, that long. And my mind drifted back to the last year of my drunkenness. I'd be alone for hours at night. Trying to write something, that's what I told myself, but by then mostly just drinking. "Come to bed earlier tonight," you'd say "it's so cold in the room without you." Or "I have such awful dreams when I dream alone." And I'd mean to come to bed earlier. I'd really mean to.

You made a list one day of all the things that would be better if I gave up the drinking.

"We'd go out together more," you were saying, "Things would be better with the kids. And you'd lose weight: maybe you'd even fit into your suit again."
"But it's up to you," you said. "If you can't do it, I won't nag you." But then you added, "I don't promise not to cry."

I knew you were right: how much more of my brain and my gut and my liver had to dissolve in the stuff? Finally, I gave it up.

"So glad you decided to stay," you said, as if it were a dinner I'd consented to, and not our lives. "You were drinking more," you said, "and looking awful. Cancelled classes when you were too hung-over to teach, and didn't seem to care. I'd get mad at you and that would only make you drink more. I wanted to shake you, I wanted to drag you out of it," you said. "But I thought it would only ruin what time we had left."

And now, forty years later, I let you suffer an extra day because I was weak and didn't want you to die.

Didn't sleep at all that night. I called the next day at the hospital, giving the miracle [(I guess) a chance to happen. Then I gave up.

They took you off the machine. They had to move you: couldn't keep you in Intensive Care, you weren't urgent anymore. There was no vacancy in the hospice. They put you in a barren little room, spare and empty but for the bed and two or three straight-backed wooden chairs, in a wing where nobody knew what to do for the dying. And Mary and Mandy and I waited. You lay unconscious, and jolted forward every twenty seconds or so with a loud, rasping breath, gulping down whatever air you could find.

"Make her comfortable," he'd said. Come and look at her now, Doctor, see if you think she's comfortable! Finally, there was a room in hospice, where you spent your last unconscious day.

And as the hours passed, I sat at your side, rooting for you to take one more breath. I was merciless, I kept trying to drag out your time.

Finally the rhythm settled into a softer beat till it ended. The music ended.

Spent the next afternoon with Mandy, picking up your things at Memory House. Afterward I walked into our house alone. Turned on the TV, the news, not because I cared right then what theater the terrorists had bombed this week, but just to hear the sound of a voice, anyone's voice. And there was the big orange tom on the couch next to the piano that hadn't been touched in two years.

I sat next to the cat, and he settled into my lap, then climbed on my chest and looked in my eyes as he used to look into yours. (Was he asking where you were?)

I brought your stuffed tiger into the house, and laid it on the sofa. Two of the cats came and sniffed at it. I convinced myself they were finding traces of you.

I slumped into my favorite chair. And wondered, before I fell asleep: what will I do with the hours I used to spend with you? And in my dream, I took you to your doctor, and the doctor didn't know you were there: couldn't see you at all. Only I could see you, and the doctor gave me papers that said you had died, and I signed. And we walked out of the doctor's office. And we took the elevator to the street and we walked down the street and you opened a handbag, and birds flew out of it, all kinds of birds, and circled over us. And I said, "How do you keep everything alive?"

Then I dreamt again, I dreamt of dreaming, of dropping off to sleep as you and I watched the news. You woke me as you always used to do: never let me sleep for long, hated doing anything alone. You woke me and we watched awhile together. I dropped off again, and when I woke, this time for real, you were gone.

Weekends after that of course were busy. People visited and told me how sorry they were for my loss and invited me for dinner, and people telephoned to ask if I was okay. Thank god it didn't last.

Dozens of people wrote condolences. Everyone remembered something you had loved: always something different. There were always things enough you loved, everybody knew one.

Mandy had said of you once, "She was up for anything. She took me to shows, she took me skiing, she took me to concerts, she took me to the Bahamas. I'd say let's do something, let's go somewhere and we'd go." Then Mandy said what many of the others have said: "She loved life".

Nowhere to turn at the house on the lake without finding you: the stuffed animals everywhere, the knick-knacks on shelves: the owl figurines, snowy owl, barn owl, great-horned owl. Your feline nativity set, with its kitten-Jesus and calico virgin and three wise toms.

You'd had it all planned, what you wanted: cremation, then the ashes in the lake. And a little gathering. We invited all the people you wanted there: Mandy and Mary and I and Mike-and-Paula from up the road, and Rolfe, old friend from your childhood, and Gail, your long-time fellow teacher and friend.

You'd picked out music for it: Vaughan Williams, The Lark Ascending. We all stood there in the living room (I don't know why nobody sat) as the violin hovered, then swooped in and out of the orchestra, then faded into the distance.

You emerged out of the shadows of people's minds. Everyone knew an anecdote.

Gail told about the time you went to a cat-show with her.
"Could you bring a carrier?" you'd asked her on the phone.
"A what?"
"A cat-carrier."
"My carriers aren't very good. Not like yours. Why don't you bring one of yours?"
"I can't."
"You *can't?*"
"No."
"Why not? And why are you whispering?"
"Larry's in the next room"
"So?"
"Just bring a carrier, okay?"
"and you can't because…"
"If he sees me with one, going out of the house, to a cat-show…"
"Oh."
"Bring one, okay?"

I hadn't heard that one. Didn't have any trouble picturing it.

We were going through the ruins of the Slingerlands house, Mandy and Mary and I.
I was amazed at how little it meant to me to see my possessions, mold-wracked, thrown into the trash: much of my library, my doctoral thesis, reprints of biological papers, magazines with my poems in them, clothing, a microscope, my clarinet. I didn't shed a tear.

Mary came upon an envelope with my name on it, in your handwriting. And gave it to me. Whether my name on it implied you meant me to find it, or only that it was somewhere to put your thoughts about me, I don't know. Mostly fragments, two or three lines at a time, observations about us, about me.

As Mary handed it to me, I remembered a time when you showed me something you had written: a poem, a nakedness, for my approval. Graceless, I read it wrong, looking for talent, looking for flaws.
I should have lifted you gentle off the pages and held you. Instead I played critic. As I read it, you were reading me. You were always good at reading someone, and I was always easy to read. You didn't show me any more poems.

You taught me how to sing. You'd have taught me how to swim and play the piano if I had let you. You taught me social graces, as much as I could learn of them – I had had none at all when we met. You taught me life is cheaper and worth a lot more (and love is easier and harder) than I'd ever known.

Not that you weren't a pain in the ass sometimes like other men's wives. Not that you never were quarrelsome, not that you didn't bitch when I watched a football game instead of raking the leaves.

Now I spend my days surrounded by your cats. I rely more and more on them. I worry about whether they like me. They're still *your* cats, they're something alive of yours. I refuse to inherit them, I'm keeping them for you. They let me into their circle of warmth. They curl up next to one another and next to me. We all lie after dark in one another's keeping.

Mandy came one weekend, and we took your dust to the lake. Mandy opened the box and freed you over the edge of the dock. Gray clouds in the shallows, billowing up off the bottom. Little fishes gathered like the ones who used to come to you at the edge of the dock, to be fed. Lake-children schooling in your shadow. You sheltered them. They welcomed you home.

After Memory House

The year you died was your eightieth year, our forty-eighth year together. And my dreams fleshed out and my days thinned to a shadow. I dream more now. Dreaming now is the chief adventure of my life.

The year you died, my worse-for-wear heart almost showed me the way to you: one valve of it gave, and the traffic slowed in the narrowing routes, and stalled and started and stalled again.

Till they laid me on the table, till somebody slit me open and held my heart in his hand and I bled away. And they gave me the blood of another man, or maybe a dozen other men: they couldn't stop the bleeding. And a part of an animal's heart. But I still had the power to dream.

While I came undone, and before they put me together again, I had, one after another, four nightmares, like four ghosts of me. Except they seemed too real for dreams, they lacked the misty nonsense, the half-baked logic of the dream. Every episode and every moment clear as waking. And in every one of them I died.
They seem now less and less like nightmares. More like prophesy.

In one, I heard the one who slit me open talking with the others. Distantly, I heard them arguing: whose fault was it? The operation botched, the patient lost. Was it the surgeon, the anesthetist, some careless nurse? I caught only a word here and there, but I knew that what they quarreled over was what I was dying of.

And in the next dream, a knowing voice, barely audible, whispered my name, and your name, and the names of our children, and gave me permission to die: "Your love is gone, your children are grown, nobody needs you now. It's all right. You can go where you need to go. Don't worry. Just rest. Be at peace." I had never been further from peace. All I could hear was his voice. He knew everything.

Another dream: I lay on a hospital bed, I lay crying for help and no help came. Attendants passed by. Coldness on their faces, blindness in their eyes. They crossed one another's path and never acknowledged one another or me. They passed my bed without seeing me. One stopped a minute near me as if he heard my call, but never looked at me and soon went on his way.

One then another exited; gradually, there were fewer and fewer till the last one left the scene. I was alone and the room grew dark.

I was transported from there into the final dream: bound, but bound to nothing, suspended in darkness, unable to move, falling into strange metamorphosis. Nausea, numbness, a sense of sinking. And the world spinning around me. But was the world spinning, or was I? No points of reference, no way to know.

I said to myself, "this must be what dying is."

Maybe, I've thought since, my surgery-dreams were akin to the final states of your mind, as if my dreams were trying to find the places where you had been.

Lately I can hardly tell one day from another. But every night is different: I never dream the same thing twice. And I remember more of my dreams than I used to. But it's not easy: I have to fight to keep a dream. Reach back for it when I wake. Right away, or I'll lose it. I sort through them in the morning to see if you're there.

I sit here sometimes during the day, sharing with you again in my mind the osprey over the lake or a deer in the yard or a giant moth at the window, or a double rainbow. Or the sight of your rag-tag garden full of wild roses and Black-eyed Susans and goldenrod and columbine.

But these last few years, I've found you mostly in dreams:

I'm sitting by your sickbed in one of my dreams.
I go to the window. Ice is falling out of the sky.
Ice is filling the streets and the yard,
ice covers the roof. The world grows slick and treacherous.
Suddenly ice is filling the room.
Then all the colors and textures of weather are swirling around us,
like strokes of the brush of an artist gone out of his mind.

You call me in one of the dreams,
to look at the dark wings hovering
birdless over the lake.
No, not wings, only the shadows of wings,
fleshless and soundless,
descending into a deep, deep dark.

I'm looking for you, riding an elevator up to
I-don't-know-what floor.
There are no buttons to push, no numbers to choose among.
I'm wandering then in a corridor,
peering into one room and another. You're nowhere.

In one dream, you let me know just what you think of what I'm writing about you. "You screwed it up," you said. "You made me too nice. You missed me completely." I explained in the dream, "You have to remember, most of this came from a young guy in love or an old man in mourning. And only a little from the middle-aged guy in between who knew you better but loved you anyway."

Your own dreams you never talked about while you were still yourself. As if you never dreamt, or never believed in your dreams. Too busy, maybe, being alive and awake.

It was only later you talked about dreams. By then you didn't know them from waking. Phantoms came to you; you taught the children among them to play the piano, and welcomed the grownups for conversation.

Some light still shone into your dwindling world. We'd be listening to music: once it was Tchaikovsky's Sixth, and you remembered the melodies: you celebrated each one as it happened, amazed and overcome by them, in love with them all over again, almost in tears: "I know that one too," you kept saying. And there was the morning one spring when you discovered the rows of bright red and orange and yellow at the back fence, and couldn't believe it:
"They're glorious! Who planted these?" you said.
"You did, Mama," Mandy told you. "You did."

The hardest time was your year at the edge, you teetering at the brink, your heart still awake, but your mind much of the time out of reach.
You were frantic one morning near Christmas: things had to be done. Presents to get for kids, checks to be sent to save-this-or-that, the children, the animals (wild and domestic), the refugees, the Redwoods. I found the addresses, labeled the envelopes, looked for the catalogues. Together we made out the checks, and found gifts that would do. By the next year, you hardly knew what Christmas and charity were.

You had seen it all coming. Your grandma had sat all afternoon in one place in your mama's house, calling over and over your mama's name. Later your own mother sat in our kitchen, commenting endlessly on the weather, noting the same stillness over and over. "Not a leaf is stirring", she'd say, whether a leaf was stirring or not.

"When I get like that," you told Mandy and me, "I want you to kill me."

And Mandy promised she would. For a minute I almost believed her. It gave you some peace I guess to think somebody would rescue you. When the time came, of course, nobody did.

God loved you without mercy when you were young: dangled enticements in front of you, gave you the heart to want and the soul to regret. When you grew old, he was still merciless.

Mandy comes down from Vermont when she can. She misses you. I remember a time when the two of you sat at the kitchen table recalling the old days. She was home for the weekend from college.
"I spoiled you," you told her
"You spoiled me rotten." she said.
"We were too close," you said
"We were. We were buddies."
"I told you too much," you said.
"You told me whatever was bothering you, and I would run and try to make it better. Long as I can remember, all I wanted was to make you happy."
You rolled your eyes "All you wanted?" you said.
"*Mostly* what I wanted."
You laughed. She in a minute laughed with you.

Mandy has the grandfather clock and the grand piano now; your mother's upright is here in the house. Out of tune. It gets dusted now and then (not by me). Otherwise nobody touches it.

Been looking at too much TV since I lost you. I think it's from spending so much time alone. Need to hear a human voice. Newscasts are best. A cat is good company, but doesn't say much.

Memory slipping away. Forgot to pay the school tax last September. And names. My god, names! I can never remember anyone's name. Even forgetting the names of animals now. The old biology prof can't remember the names of animals.

And last autumn, the house was invaded. One horde of flies, then another. Enough to make an old man believe in omens.

In August the flesh flies, the big ones, scores of them all at once, hurtled through rooms, buzzing near windows. As if something had already died here.

In September the little ones, hundreds of them, and more arriving every hour, accumulating on the walls. Looking back, they were well-mannered little flies. Didn't buzz around your head. Didn't go browsing through dinner. But at the time, their silence and patience were a little unnerving, especially while their numbers kept growing. At night, as I moved from one room to another, they followed the light through the house. I felt pursued.

Threatened, I formulated a plan: I first turned every light out but the one in the living room, and after they'd gathered there, I went to the vestibule and turned that one on, and turned the one in the living room off. And then we went up the stairway, with the light on at the top of the stairs. Finally only the light in the spare bedroom was still on, and gradually most of the flies made their way there, and I closed the door behind them. Not sure what I was trying to save myself from. But it was comforting somehow to have most of the little harbingers out of sight.

I don't think I dreamt that. I think it really happened.

"Take care of my kitties," you used to tell me.

In the years since I promised, we've lost all but one. Nefret and I are still here looking after each other. She's someone to talk to, and fuss over and worry about.

We lost Clara to cancer a while back. Had I told you that? Clara remembered you, I think, right to the last: something about her body remembered your body. She would sit with me sometimes, but her manner told me it just wasn't the same.

Big Guy just collapsed in a corner one night. Kidneys, they think. Too calm here without him. He was the same sort of person you were. Forever stirring things up, making trouble, shattering every peace I had thought I wanted. Going to miss him.

Buttons and I went to the Vet and found out about all the awful things that were happening in him: they listed nearly every part of him. He died nearly a year after the vet had declared him hopeless. I held him as they put the needle in and set him free.

I've been losing you again, one cat at a time.

You'd have loved the colors of the sky today. I'm always finding something in a day or season you'd have loved. You used to call me this time of year to help you celebrate the grand openings: lilacs, say, or lilies or roses. The wisteria you brought with us from Albany is overrunning the place. Grabbing at every trunk and stick and stem. It's covering the yard, hugging the house and garage, and waving tendrils at unwary passers-by.

Marge-next-door has died. Two of those great water-colors of hers are still hanging here in the living room. Toward the end, I went to see her; she hadn't left her house in weeks.
"Just stopped by to say hello," I meant to say to her, but said instead (slip of the tongue, slip of the mind) "to say goodbye".
I was horrified, but she nodded and smiled as if to thank me for saying what nobody else would say.

A pileated woodpecker, a bird you would have adored, has annihilated one of the maples out front: just as well, it was rotting out. One more of the maples is in trouble, leafy as it still is in summer. Tree people wanted to take it down. I wouldn't let them: It's an old friend, let it fall of its own weight, like the rest of us. The ginkgo at the edge of the porch is making a comeback.

There's only one bird feeder now, I'm afraid. I fill it when I remember.

Your mail has never stopped. Some piano sheet-music just arrived. I keep hearing the ghosts of Chopin and Debussy, and the stuff you had the kids play. All the catalogues keep coming too, Paragon, Bits and Pieces, Jackson and Perkins, and all the rest, that I used to bring you in November to get you to pick out some things you liked, to give me something to get you for Christmas, because I was so bad at picking things out.

You're still a paid-up member of the ACLU. It's still in your name. You're still a champion of the rights of people against tyranny.

When Mandy and I laid your dust in the lake, the waterlilies and the curly-weeds were already at the water's edge. No need to clear them away: nobody would be swimming there. Out on the dock, moments we'd spent there together came back to me, you swimming or sunning, I with a camera, photographing you and the lake and the geese and the dragonflies.

I found the other day a photo of you from a time near the end at Memory House. There's a blankness on your face, there's a personlessness in your eyes. But holding your big plush tiger tight to your breast. You loved your tiger. And you still loved the colors of flowers, you still loved a song, you still loved people and were forever telling them so.
Though I wonder now: how much of I-love-you was love and how much of it fear?

Before I saw you die, I thought I knew what death was: I didn't. I knew that death was final, but I didn't know what final was. But I knew, the day you died. I haven't known since, but the day you died, I knew.

I go on writing, as if I think you'll materialize if I just put down enough words. Any year now, or for all I know any day, I'll run out of words. Dreams will be what I've got left. And maybe I'll know them from waking. Or maybe my dreams and waking will merge the way yours did, and I'll dream you back into someplace where only I will see you and hear you. There will be your garden and the cats and the lake and the lilacs, and maybe we'll spend an hour together, and maybe you'll know my name again.

www.ingramcontent.com/pod-product-compliance
Lightning Source LLC
LaVergne TN
LVHW041545070526
838199LV00046B/1838